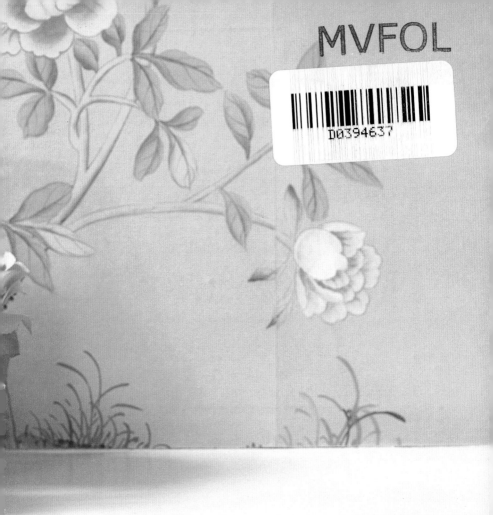

MVFOL

mad about

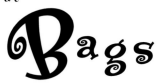

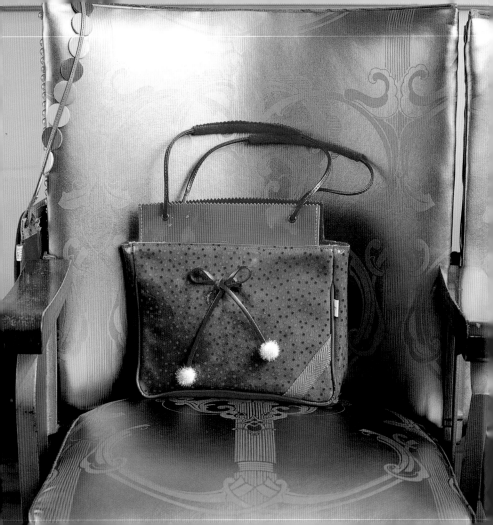

mad about

Bags

Emma Bowd

RYLAND
PETERS
& SMALL
LONDON NEW YORK

Designer Luis Peral-Aranda
Editor Miriam Hyslop
Location Research Manager Kate Brunt
Production Tamsin Curwood
Art Director Gabriella Le Grazie
Publishing Director Alison Starling

First published in the United States in 2002
by Ryland Peters & Small, Inc.
519 Broadway
5th Floor
New York NY 10012
www.rylandpeters.com

10 9 8 7 6 5 4 3 2

Printed and bound in China

Library of Congress Cataloging-in-Pubication-Data

Bowd, Emma.
  Mad about bags / by Emma Bowd.
    p. cm.
  ISBN 1-84172-355-X
  1. Handbags. I. Title.

GT2180 .B69 2002
391.4'1—dc21   2002066760

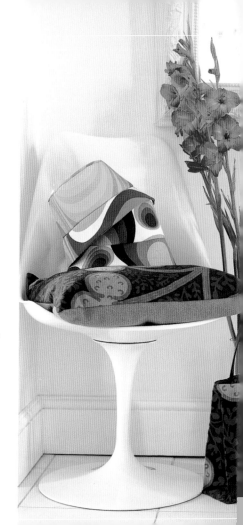

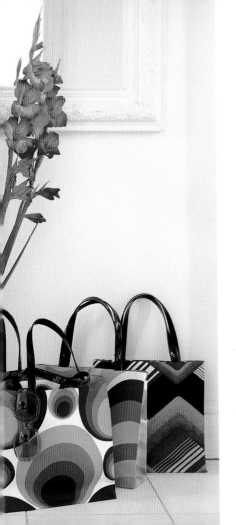

contents

Handbags are hypnotic, spell-binding little creatures that entice a significant number of women into their world. The sheer volume of them in our closets is testament to the fact that we seem to be totally incapable of resisting the seduction of their charms.

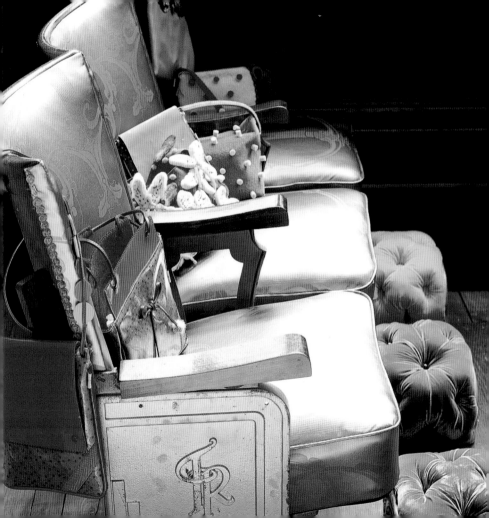

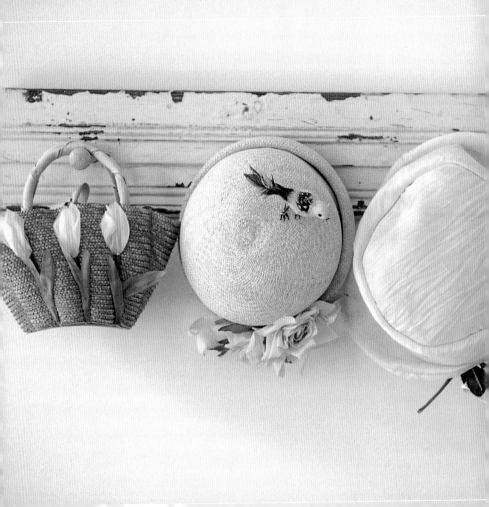

first handbags

*H*andbags are grown-up versions of our childhood fascination with all brightly colored objects that glisten and gleam, open and close, and sparkle and sway. It is a fact, deplored by those politically correct new mothers, that darling little girls will almost always choose the pretty pink, fluffy, sequined Barbie handbag over the ergonomically designed and environmentally friendly toddler backpack. And handbag designers know that we never grow out of this! They constantly lure us with a seemingly endless array of shiny clasps, slinky straps, bold buckles, exotic textures, prettily patterned fabrics, beading, stitching, and magical secret chambers.

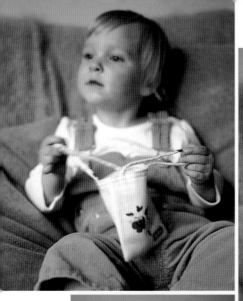
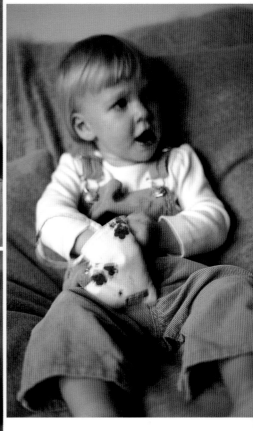
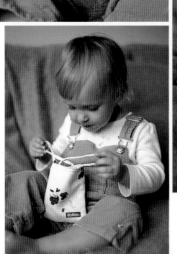

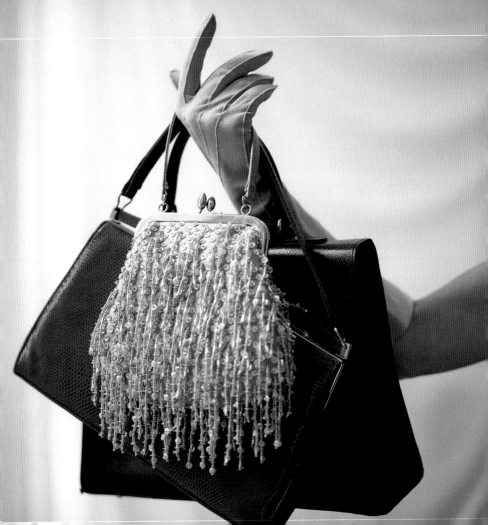

one size fits all

Any diehard handbag lover knows only too well the pleasure of purchasing a gorgeous, gleaming handbag. The mere fact that the two of you are joined in this happy union gives you instant, calorie-free joy. Moreover, you don't need to worry about trying it on with fingers and toes crossed in the vain hope that it will fit you. Handbags never let you down! Whether your style is tote or clutch, vintage or cutting edge, chain store or Chanel, your stunning new handbag will be admired and envied long before anyone notices the size of your thighs or the bad hair day you may be experiencing. What better fashion accessory could a woman want?

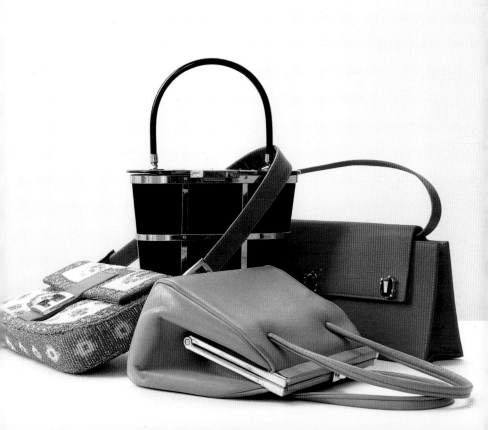

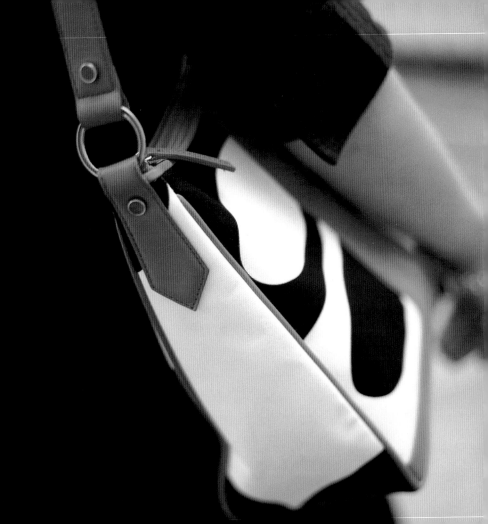

big is beautiful

The appeal of handbags rests in the very fact that they are beautiful, so they make us feel beautiful. Their outward appearance allows us to maintain a certain semblance of fashion credibility, too, irrespective of whether inside nestles a silk Fendi makeup bag and gold embossed Filofax or diary, or half-eaten toddler rusks and baby wipes. No one need ever be the wiser! And the bigger our handbags are, the more we can hide inside them. We all have friends who carry around what could easily amount to their entire life's belongings in their trusty sacks, ready for whatever eventuality may come their way. Or, if you are a Parisian,

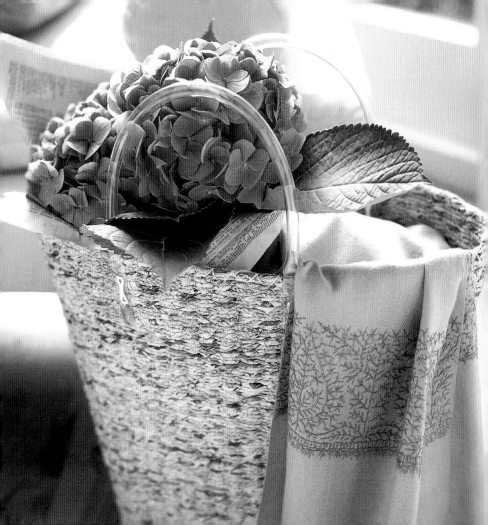

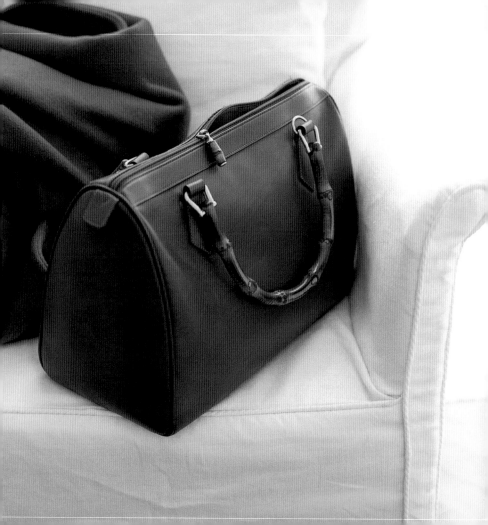

it may be your perfectly coiffed pet poodle that takes pride of position in your handbag! Many of us have a big, loyal work bag, too. This is the one constant companion that is never far from our sides, with all the lumps, bumps, and scratches to prove its

bags of style

devotion. These bags meet our needs so perfectly, in both the fashion and function stakes, that we find it hard to live without them. They always have good solid straps that are undeniably comfortable to wear for long periods of time and durable enough to withstand being jostled and jammed in rush hour crowds. A secure zip to deter prying hands is almost always a pre-requisite. The fact that it effortlessly matches numerous pairs of shoes (both winter and summer) adds further to its longevity as your number one bag. Usually, no matter how many times we try to substitute another handbag for our current long-standing work bag, we always end up returning to the same old faithful friend. At times, we will need to employ the operation of a "dual handbag" system, whereby we take an additional, smaller, and more fashionable handbag to work with us for important lunchtime meetings and romantic evening dinner dates.

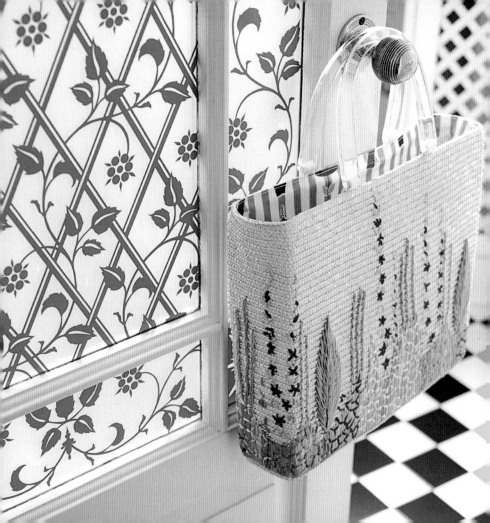

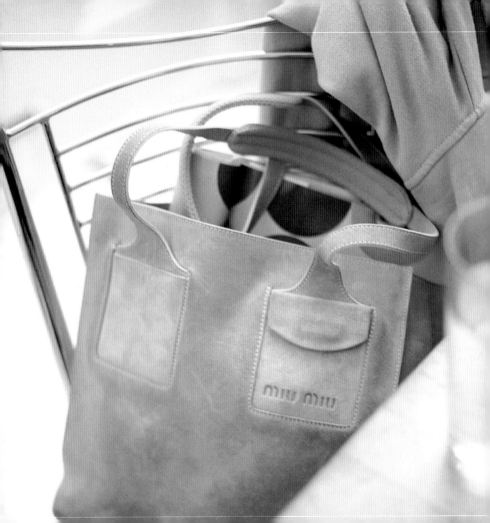

the favorite bag

Most of us can admit to having one special handbag amid the masses in the closet that has the esteemed status of being the favorite. This type of purse has many guises, changing shape and color from season to season, month to month, or even week to week depending on our latest whim. Your "current" favorite is usually a very beautiful handbag that instantly transforms last season's outfits with its up-to-the-minute styling and colors. Like the tangerine and pink felt bowling bag from a cutting-edge new designer, which is the perfect size to carry the exact amount of items you need to survive your day. Or the brilliant fire-engine red mock-croc

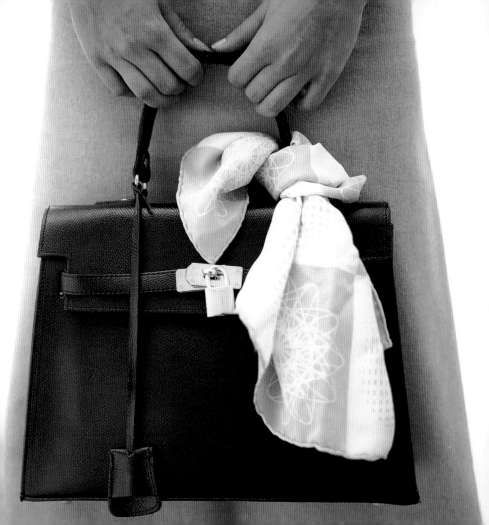

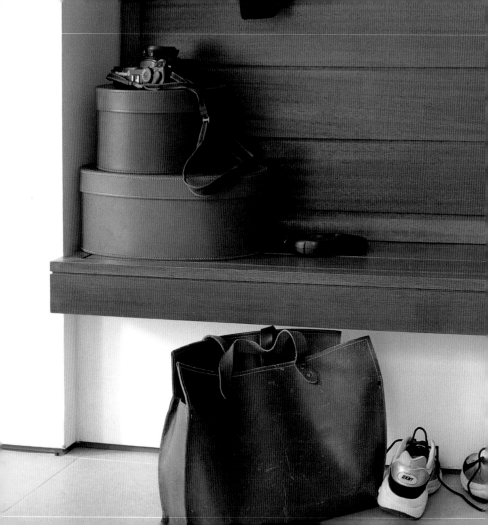

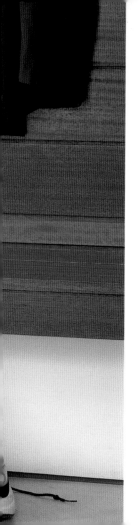

shoulder bag with pencil-thin straps that makes those long mid winter days so much more bearable. It could also be the huge tote bag that goes everywhere with you, whose versatility provides seamless transitions between office, gym, lunch dates, and shopping trips. And it is always exciting when you delve into the abyss of its inner reaches only to discover a favorite lipstick that you haven't seen in months! Or, your favorite handbag may very well be the bag that has never actually seen active duty on your arm, spending its days making your dressing table look beautiful, instead. Like the exquisitely beaded evening bag, which caught your eye on the sale counter of an expensive store, that you could not walk past because it was your favorite color and when you looked at the label it was actually named after you. For the truly besotted handbag lover, the all-time favorite handbag is no more than an elusive dream. A handbag so desired that waiting lists of up to six months are the norm. Some handbags, like the coveted Kelly bag, even require you to be invited onto the list. Surely it is the goal of every obsessed bag lover to own such a bag!

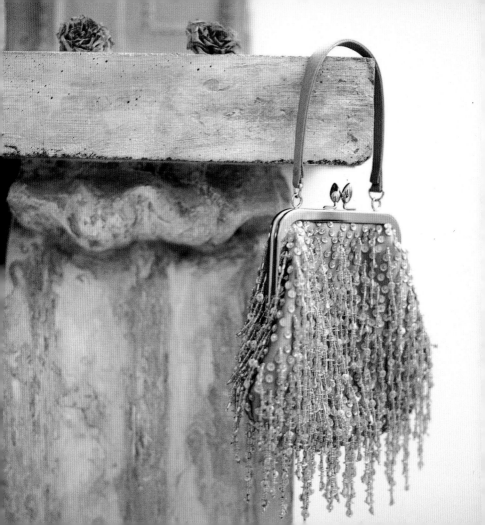

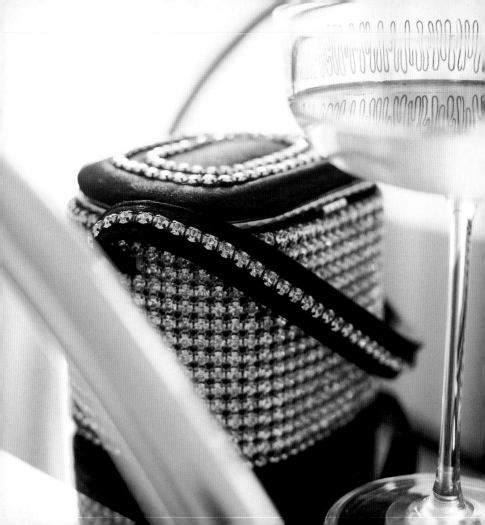

the evening bag

Evening bags personify the sheer indulgence, beauty, and glamour of the special occasion you have gone to all the trouble of attending. Their sole purpose is to be the jewel in the crown of your outfit. Make sure you relish every moment of such a rare and exciting opportunity to delve into this exotic, fabulously feathered world. And the more silk, satin, and sequins used the better. Whether you opt for a crystal-encrusted clutch, a slinky metallic mesh pouch, or something dainty with bejeweled handles or gleaming clasps, you will be sure to sparkle all night long. But most of all, the size of your evening bag must not be much bigger than a tube of lip-

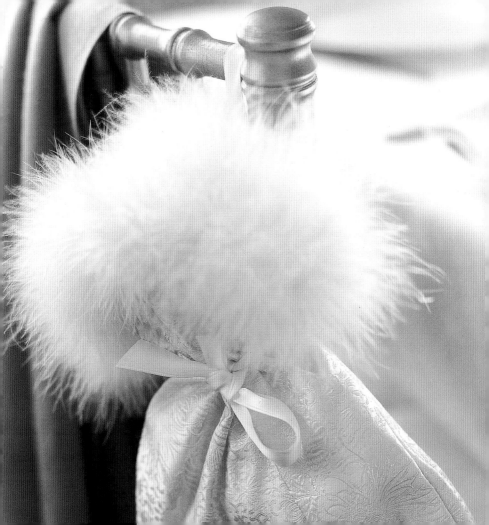

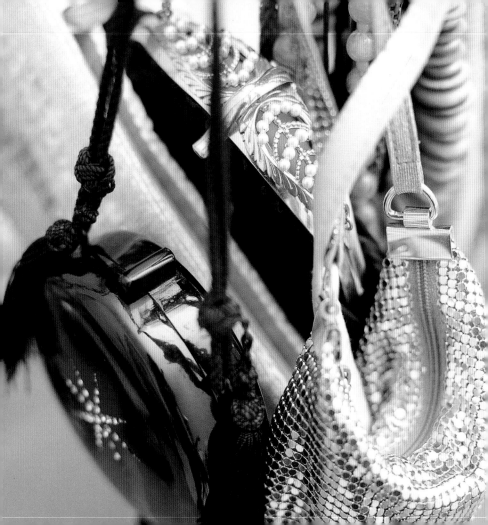

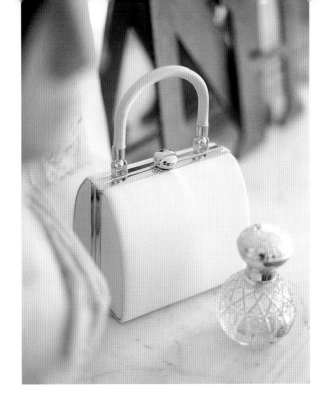

stick. You will, of course, be compelled
to squeeze your extra bits and pieces
into your partner's suit pocket!

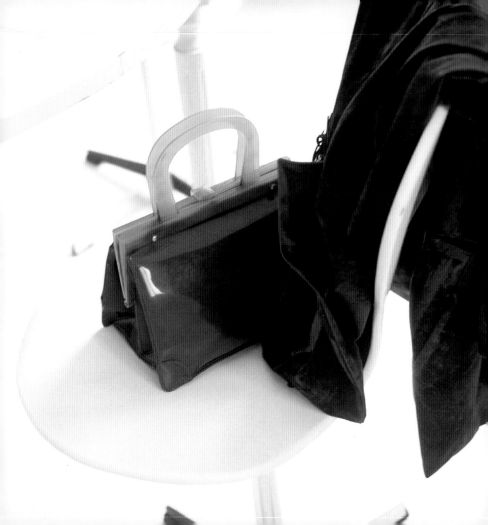

the vintage bag

There is one very big advantage to painstakingly looking after your handbags and storing them away when they're out of date. If you keep them long enough and resurrect them at just the right time, they enter the hallowed arena of the "vintage handbag." Vintage bags ooze class, confidence, and style. Don't cave in to the pressures of feng shui by throwing out all of those piles of handbags in the top of your closet. Instead, pack them up and forget about them for 20 years. Your daughters will love you for it when today's fashion goes through the inevitable "retro" phase, and they will have an enviable collection of delightful vintage handbags to choose from

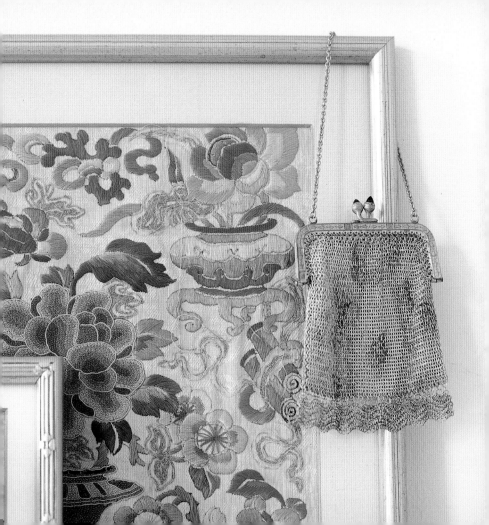

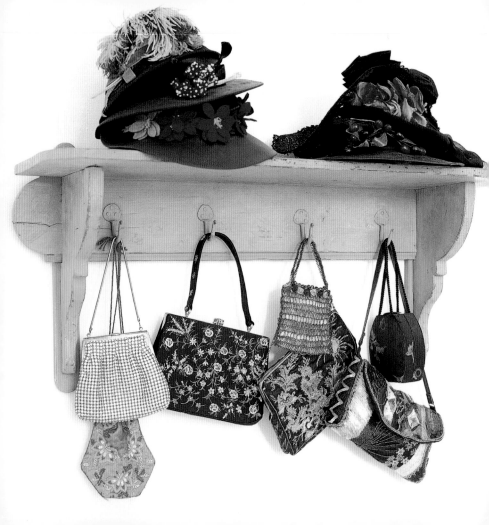

What more beautiful family heirloom could a girl ask for? A passion for vintage handbags can also provide us with very special experiences, like the magical thrill of rummaging through an obscure thrift shop and stumbling upon the most exquisite handbag you

timeless treasures

have ever seen. And of course there is the fascinating speculation about what sort of life your discovery may have had before your paths crossed. The owner, the parties, the dresses, the shoes—all a truly unique mystery and mystique that lives on forever.

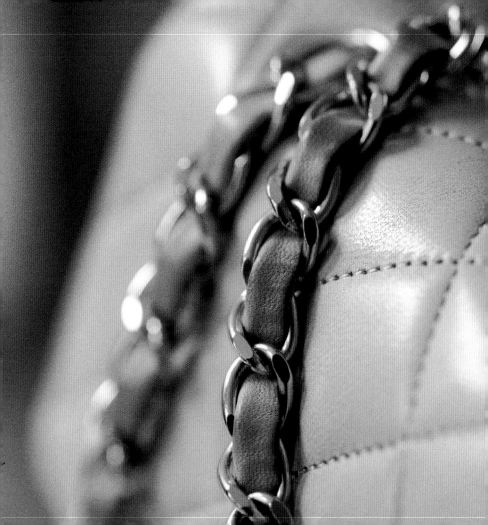

the designer bag

The dedicated handbag lover will usually succumb to at least one of the three popular types of designer handbag. First, there is the obvious logo-emblazoned handbag that announces to the world, in all its bold glory, your immediate membership of a very special club. Logos range from discreet metal clasps to boldly tattooed symbols that cover the bag. Importantly, these handbags are also the only fashion items in our wardrobes which make it acceptable, even desirable, to arrive at a party carrying an identical accessory to that of someone else. Second, there is the handbag produced by the talented, upscale designer who has carved out a certain

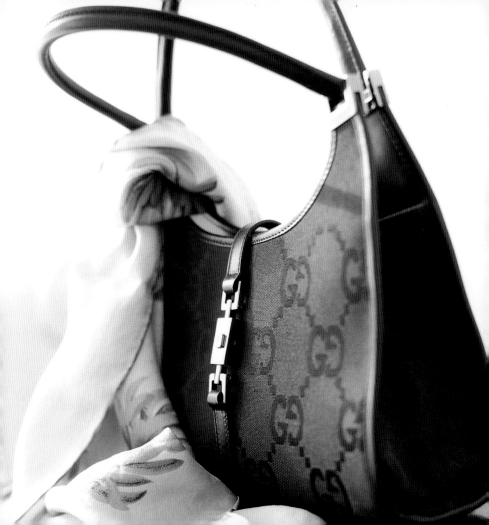

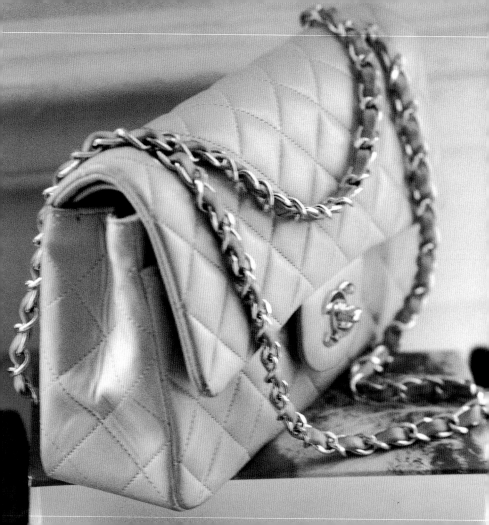

"look" or "style," without the need for visible logos. This type of bag certainly sorts out the true handbag devotees from the logo junkies, and is always greatly admired and appreciated for its subtle beauty. The third type of designer handbag is the "one-off" handmade

crème de la crème

variety—the crème de la crème of handbags—that are unique in their design and exquisite in their craftsmanship. They are living displays of the artisan's skills in the use of materials and leave the mass-produced bags lagging a long way behind in any competition.

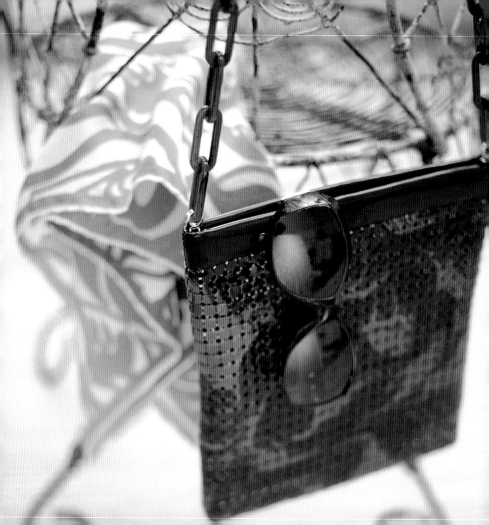

the vacation bag

The most exciting part about packing for your long-anticipated summer vacation is rummaging through the deepest depths of your closet to choose which one of the seven "vacation" bags (all bought on previous trips) you will take with you. Whether it's your Biarritz market canvas carry-all, or your woven raffia Guatemalan beach basket, these bags are characteristically cavernous in size. And they all remind you of sunny, carefree times abroad in exotic locations. If you find the prospect of lugging a huge rustic bag through city airport check-ins too daunting, then there are always the upscale designers to save the day with their stunning collections

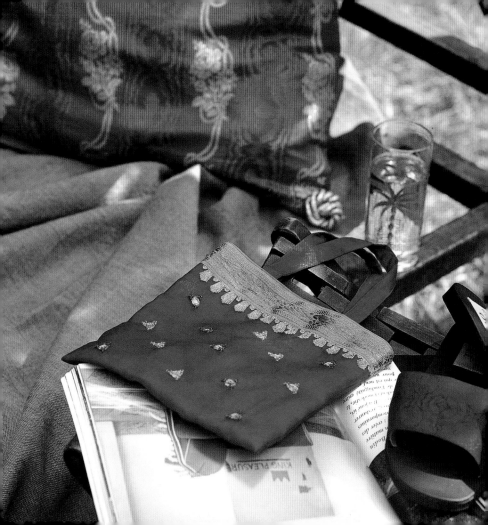

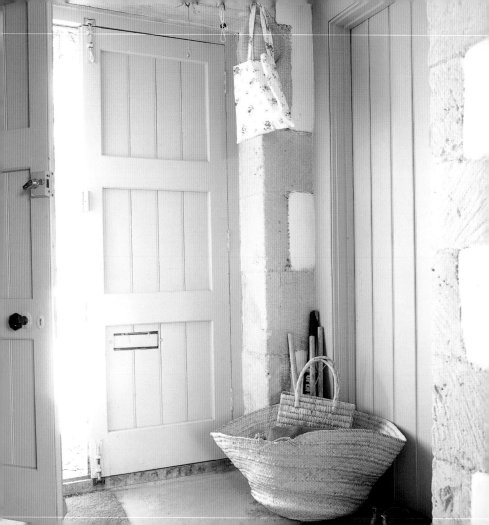

of vacation bags. These bags are the centerpiece of the chic beach vacation wardrobe. From these collections you can create a vast array of seamless ensembles—perfectly matching shoes, bikinis, sarongs, and hats—which will help you blend in effortlessly to that

handbag therapy

fashionable St. Tropez boulevard. The ultimate European destination for the handbag devotee is a weekend of shameless retail therapy in Florence, Italy. Allow plenty of space in your case and you can return home with a divine assortment of elegant bags!

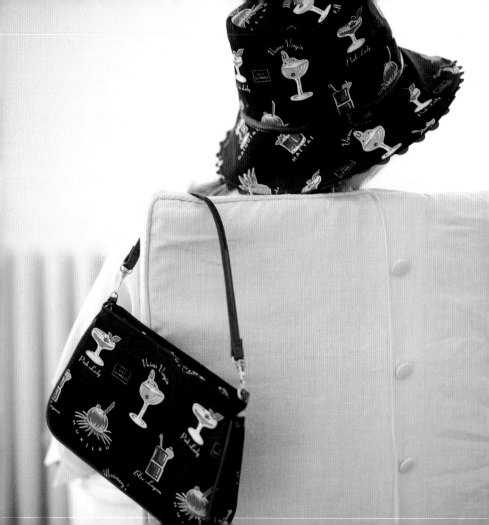

the perfect match

Every handbag fan knows only too well that bags are an integral part of our female social fabric. The vast array of colors, shapes, textures, and styles at our fingertips means that no day need go by without the best handbag to complement our current mood, age, and budget—from solid, square power bags, to slinky, mesh evening bags, timeless couture treasures, and savvy, streetwise totes. At last, handbag designers have figured out that when we go shopping to buy a coffeepot, we often come home with a yellow daisy-appliquéd "bag of the season" instead! Whatever the life event, you can be sure that a suitably noteworthy handbag is at the

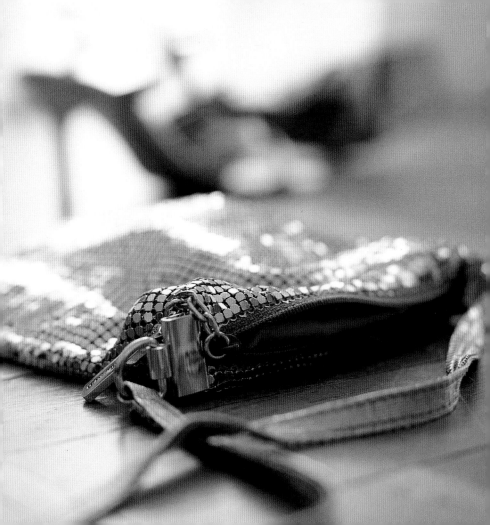

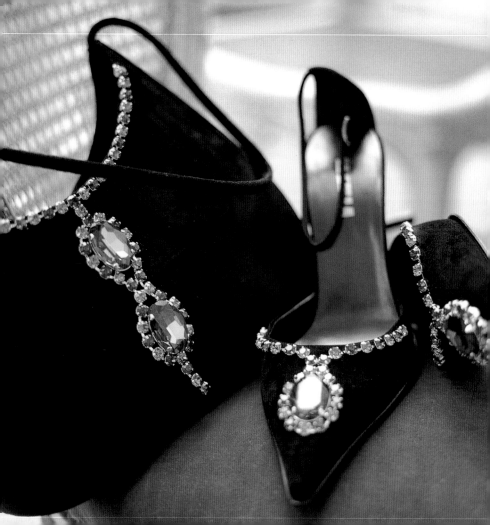

center of your memories. Like dancing around them in discos with a gaggle of girlfriends, blowing your first "real" paycheck on a "must-have" designer bag or attending your first glittering black-tie ball. When occasion calls, rarely is an eyebrow raised at the indulgent

decadence

purchase of a gorgeous black-suede rhinestone-encrusted handbag with shoes and belt to match. And what better way to make a statement of coordinated wedding chic than by commissioning a made-to-order hat and handbag from your favorite designer? Pure decadence!

suppliers & stockists

Anthropologie
85 South 5th Avenue
New York
NY 10003-3002
t. 800 543 1039 for stores
www.anthropologie.com

Anya Hindmarsh
www.beabag.com

Barneys New York
660 Madison Avenue
New York
NY 10019
t. 212 826 8900
www.barneys.com

Bergdorf Goodman
754 5th Avenue
New York
NY 10019
t. 212 753 7300

Bill Amberg
230 Elizabeth Street
New York
NY 10012
t. 212 625 8556
www.billamberg.com

Bloomingdale's
1000 Third Avenue
New York
NY 10022
www.bloomingdales.com

Chanel
15 East 57th Street
New York
NY 10022
t. 800 550 0005 for stores
www.chanel.com

Christian Dior
t. 800 929 DIOR for stores
www.dior.com

Coach
t. 800 444 3611 for stores
www.coach.com

Fendi
t. 800 FENDI-NY for stores

Furla
727 Madison Avenue
New York 10021-8003
t. 212 755 8986
www.furla.com

Gucci
685 Fifth Avenue
New York
NY 10022
t. 212 826 2600
www.gucci.com

Hèrmes
691 Madison Avenue
New York
NY 10012
t. 800 441 4488 for stores
www.hermes.com

Kate Spade
454 Broome Street
New York
NY 10012
t. 212 274 1991
www.katespade.com

Linda Bee
Grays Antique Market
26 South Molton Lane
London W1K 5AB
England
t. 00 44 (0)20 7629 5921

Longchamp
713 Madison Avenue
New York
NY 10021
t. 212 223 1500
www.longchamp.com

Louis Vuitton
t. 866 VUITTON for stores
www.louisvuitton.com

Lulu Guinness
394 Bleecker Street
New York
NY 10012
t. 212 367 2120
www.luluguinness.com

Macy's
151 West 34th Street
New York
NY 10001–2101
t. 212 695 4400
www.macys.com

Neiman Marcus
t. 800 365 7989 for stores
www.neimanmarcus.com

Parallel
22 Marylebone High Street
London W1M 3PE
England
t. +44 (0)20 7224 0441

Prada
t. 888 977 1900 for stores

Saks Fifth Avenue
611 Fifth Avenue
New York
NY 10022
t. 212 753 4000
www.saksfifthavenue.com

credits & acknowledgments

key: *a*=above, *b*=below, *l*=left, *r*=right, *c*=center

Special photography: Chris Everard
Other photography by:
Chris Drake: *53*
Chris Everard: *8; 14; 16; 19; 20; 24; 27; 30; 32; 36; 37; 47; 50; 56; 59; 60*
Catherine Gratwicke: *2 & 7* VV Rouleaux, Ribbons, Trimmings, and Braids; *4-5* Martin
Barrell and Amanda Sellers' flat, owners of Maisonette, London; *23 & 41; 42* Lulu
Guiness's house in London
Tom Leighton: *38*
Debi Treloar: *12* Ben John's and Deb Waterman, John's house in Georgetown
Pia Tryde: *44; 48*
Alan Williams: *54*
Andrew Wood: *28*
Polly Wreford: *10; 35*

Huge thanks to Fiona for sharing her divine collection of handbags (and hat!) with the
world. We're all jealous!

The author and publisher would also like to thank everyone who made the photography
for this book possible. Grateful thanks to Parallel and Linda Bee for loaning items for
photography.

Special thanks to Debbie, Emma, Darcey, and to Jo Blyth, and little Emily for modelling.

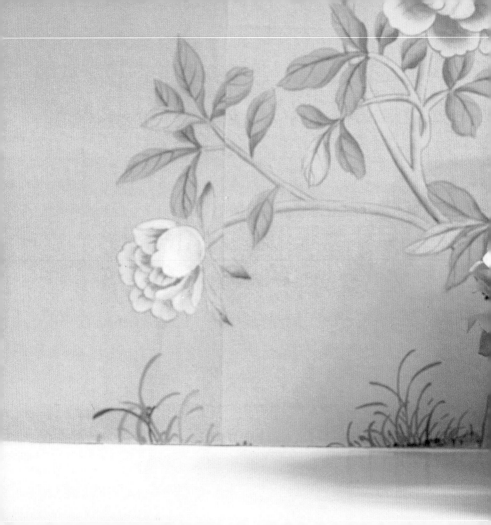